D1060795

779.25
R21
4.88
70628

My Friends Live in Many Places

DORKA RAYNOR

Albert Whitman & Company, Chicago

With loving memory of my brother Artek,
and that never-forgotten evening of our childhood when,
both of us crying, he valiantly and unsuccessfully
tried to shield me with his body
from the only spanking my father ever gave me.
I understood even then the justice of this spanking,
for my father loved me, and I had broken the rules for my safety.

Artek died in the uprising of the Warsaw ghetto
on Monday, April 4, 1943. With this dedication
he will live for a while in the minds
of those who read these lines.

And for Lilah.

Library of Congress Cataloging in Publication Data
Raynor, Dorka.
    My friends live in many places.
    (A Concept book)
    SUMMARY: Photographs record the activities of
children in many different countries.
    1. Children—Pictorial works—Juvenile literature.
[1. Manners and customs—Pictorial works] I. Title.
HQ781.5.R39   779'.25   79-27655
ISBN 0-8075-5353-0 lib. bdg.

COPYRIGHT© 1980 BY DORKA RAYNOR
PUBLISHED SIMULTANEOUSLY IN CANADA
BY GENERAL PUBLISHING, LIMITED, TORONTO
ALL RIGHTS RESERVED.
PRINTED IN THE UNITED STATES OF AMERICA.

2 Shepherds, France

3 Jardin des Plantes, Paris, France

4 Child with mola, Isla Wichub-Wala, Panama

5 Circus child, Mérida, Mexico

6 Coming home from school, Hong Kong

7 Morocco

9 Dublin, Ireland

8 Tehran, Iran

10　Tokyo, Japan

13　At the market, Tomar, Portugal

12　Village festival, Sakamoto, Japan

14   Mourners at the cemetery, Nassau, Bahamas

16   Blessing of the animals, San Antonio Day, Mexico City, Mexico

18   Tending her cattle, Atlas Mountains, Morocco

19   Crete, Greece

20   Katmandu, Nepal

26 Tokyo, Japan

27 Lilah in Chicago, United States

28   Wedding guest, Avignon, France

30 Bride and groom, Saas-Fée, Switzerland

31 Wedding guests, Quiberon, France

32   Girls' school, Madrid, Spain

33   Denpasar, Bali, Indonesia

34 Nassau, Bahamas

35 Neapolitan boys in Rome, Italy

36   Saas-Fée, Switzerland

38   Boy eating sugar cane, Egypt

39   Bombay, India

I want to grow up ... not blow up
Let's MAKE CHICAGO
LITTER PERFECT
SANITATION CHICAGO

41 La Feria, Seville, Spain

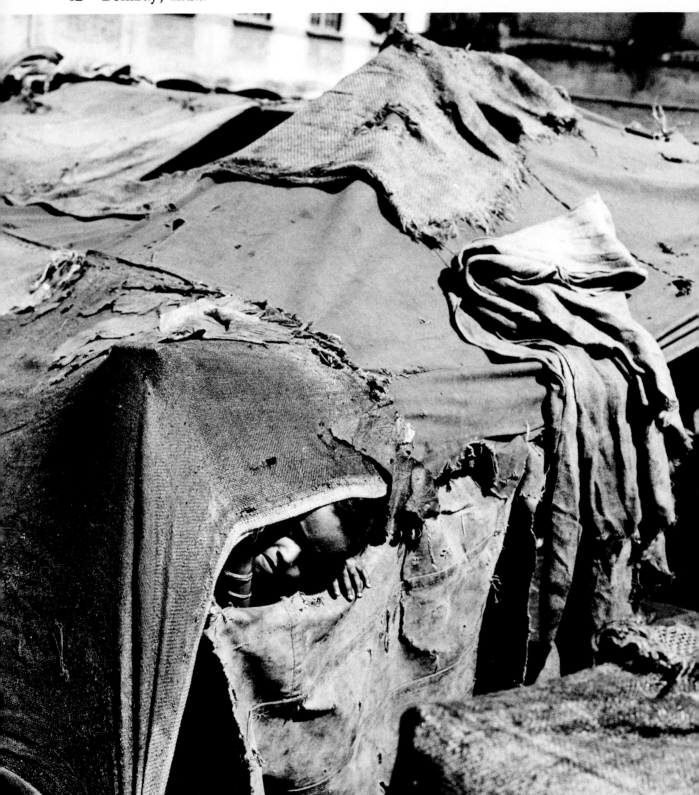

43   France

70628

44 Charles de Gaulle Airport, Paris, France

45 Eiffel Tower, Paris, France

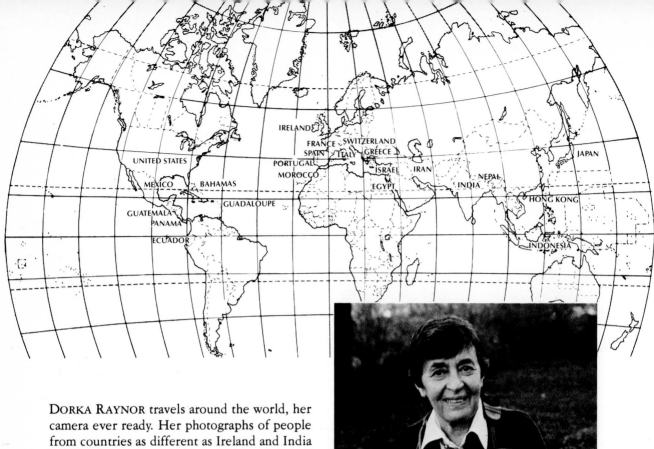

Marc Hauser

DORKA RAYNOR travels around the world, her camera ever ready. Her photographs of people from countries as different as Ireland and India have appeared in many textbooks and in two of her own collections, *This Is My Father and Me* and *Grandparents Around the World,* both published by Albert Whitman. Prints in this book found in permanent museum collections are numbers 2 and 43, from the Art Institute of Chicago, and number 3, from the Metropolitan Museum of Art, New York City. Mrs. Raynor has been honored by the American Society of Magazine Photographers and awarded prizes in France.

Writing to Mrs. Raynor about her photographs, A. Hyatt Mayor, former curator of the Metropolitan Museum of Art, said, "You are a force of joy in this age of apprehension. The world cannot be heading for quite such a catastrophe when you find the same exquisite communion in all costumes and in all lands. You have created a treasure of variety in unity."

COUNTRIES PICTURED

70628

C
779.25
R21

Date Due

MAY 25 1982	NOV 28 1995		
MAR 0 1 1983	APR 1 1 1998		
MAY 24 1983	FEB 20		
MAR 2 0 1984	FE 16 01		
MAY 15 1984	UV 01 03		
OCT 3 0 1984			
JAN 08 1985			
FEB 12 1986			
APR 2 1 1987			
APR 1 3 1998			

NYACK COLLEGE LIBRARY
NYACK, NEW YORK